Jack Johnson
In Between Dreams

CONTENTS

Transcribed by Jeff Jacobson

Cherry Lane Music Company
Director of Publications/Project Editor: Mark Phillips

ISBN 1-57560-830-8

Visit our website at www.cherrylane.com

Jack Johnson — In Between Dreams

In the past five years, Jack Johnson has gone from filmmaker, shooting and scoring his 16mm surf films, to well-known singer/songwriter. After spending 2003 on the road in support of *On and On*, and slowing down in 2004 to welcome his new baby boy, Johnson has released his third and most musically upbeat release to date, *In Between Dreams*.

Raised on the Hawaiian island of Oahu, Johnson practically began to surf as he began to walk. As the youngest of three wave-riding brothers and a long-boarding father, most of Johnson's life lessons were learned in the water. With Pipeline in his front yard, Johnson started surfing the legendary wave at age 12. At 17 he was invited to surf in the Pipe Masters competition, and one month later he suffered a surfing accident that kept him out of the water for three months. Although Johnson had began playing guitar as a young teen, it was those land-locked months that allowed Johnson to hone his guitar skills and find influences in a wide range of musicians, from Cat Stevens to Fugazi.

At 18 Johnson left the Islands to study filmmaking at the University of California at Santa Barbara. After graduating in 1997, he began a year-long adventure around the world with old surfing friends Chris and Emmett Malloy. The result was the acclaimed 16mm surf film *Thicker Than Water*, which was hailed as a return to the purist beauty of early surf cinema and which Johnson co-directed and shot. It was during the scoring of the film that Johnson found his musical voice. Before its release in 1999, Johnson's soulful folk tunes, inflected with blues and hip-hop flavorings, soon began circulating as bootlegs in all corners of the global surf community.

At this time Johnson met fellow surfer Garrett Dutton (aka G. Love), who recorded Johnson's "Rodeo Clowns" for the G. Love & Special Sauce disc *Philadelphonic*, also released in 1999. The recording quickly gained radio airplay and Johnson's reputation as a musician began to grow beyond the surf community. Despite offers to sign a record deal, Johnson chose to escape to the South Pacific to film his second surf film, *The September Sessions*. By the time *Thicker Than Water* was named *Surfer* magazine's Film of the Year and its follow-up, *The September Sessions*, nabbed the Adobe Highlight Award at the ESPN Film Festival, Johnson's bootleg tape fell into the hands of musician Ben Harper and his manager/producer J.P. Plunier, who helped Johnson make a record.

In January 2001 Johnson's full-length debut, *Brushfire Fairytales*, was released on Enjoy Records, an upstart indie label founded by veteran A&R man Andy Factor and Plunier, who produced the recording. *Brushfire Fairytales* was an impressive debut on numerous levels: From the opening "Inaudible Melodies"—which seemed to boil down Jack's personal philosophy to a chorus of "Slow down everyone/You're moving too fast"— to the anthemic "Flake," *Brushfire Fairytales* turned on many people across the nation to Jack Johnson. While opening for Ben Harper's four-month U.S./Australian tour in 2001, *Brushfire Fairytales* started to build momentum and spread like wildfire among the enthusiastic, music-minded Harper crowd. By the fall, Johnson, drummer Adam Topol, and bassist Merlo Podlewski were selling out their own club shows. Within a year of the album's release it had sold 100,000

copies; in January 2003 it went platinum.

In May 2003, Johnson released his sophomore album, *On and On*, which was produced by Mario Caldato, Jr., best known for his work with the Beastie Boys, and which featured the same lineup as *Brushfire Fairytales*: Jack on vocals/guitar, Adam Topol on drums, and Merlo Podlewski on bass. *On and On* mixed heartfelt ballads of love and simple joys with more serious subjects of materialism, industrialization, school shootings, offshore oil drilling, and war. The inner truth and social commentary that was evident in Johnson's early songwriting on *Brushfire Fairytales* matured with *On and On*.

On and On's release launched Johnson's newly formed Brushfire Records label and garnered sales of one million within its first year. Also during that year Brushfire Records welcomed Jack's old friends G. Love and Donavon Frankenreiter, a professional surfer/musician, and released the soundtracks for Johnson's surf films, *Thicker Than Water* and *The September Sessions*.

In March 2005 Johnson released his third full-length recording, *In Between Dreams*. Acoustic sing-a-longs full of smartly embellished strumming and solid bass lines create a hypnotic, blues- and funk-inflected groove that flows through the album. *In Between Dreams* was recorded in Hawaii and Los Angeles and was produced by Mario Caldato, Jr., and engineered by Robert Carranza—the same duo at the controls for 2003's *On and On*. *In Between Dreams* also features contributions from Jack's friend Zach Gill (Animal Liberation Orchestra) on piano and accordion.

The songs on *In Between Dreams* are nostalgic and romantic. "Better Together," with its boxes of photographs awash in "sepia-toned lovin'," is a love song Johnson penned for his wife, Kim: "It's not always easy and sometimes life can be deceiving/But I'll tell you one thing: it's always better when we're together." The upbeat "Staple It Together" reminds us to roll with life's punches, while "If I Could," quietly laced with melodica and hand drums, is a heartfelt goodbye to a friend: "I heard some words from a friend on the phone that didn't sound so good/The doctor gave him two weeks to live/I'd give him more, if I could." Some tracks, like the accordion-filled "Bella," predate *Brushfire Fairytales*, while others, like "Crying Shame," were written just as the album was being finished. The first single track, "Sitting, Waiting, Wishing," is about a friend's amusing pursuit of a girl.

Having started playing music at his family barbecues and atop boats on far-off surf trips, it must be a touch surreal when Johnson finds himself traveling the world with his band, performing on television shows, and playing to sold-out amphitheatres. But the reality is that Jack Johnson has accomplished an impressive amount over the last few years as an artist, filmmaker, musician, and now as a father. His third full-length release, *In Between Dreams*, delivers his signature sound that fans around the world have grown to love in an upbeat collection of songs that will get everyone to sing along.

BETTER TOGETHER

Words and Music by
Jack Johnson

Intro
Moderately ♩ = 112

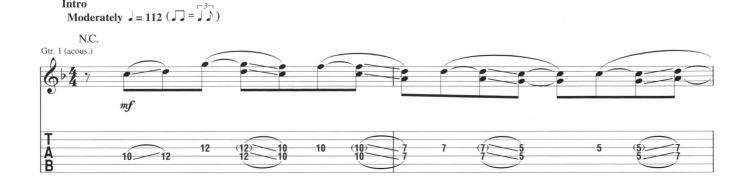

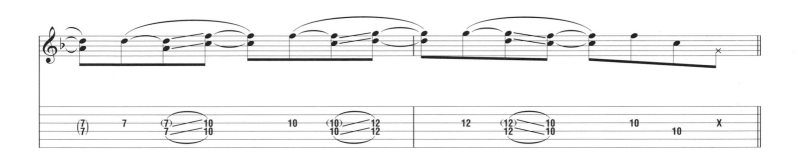

Verse

2nd time, Gtr. 2: w/ Fill 1

F   F/E   Dm   C

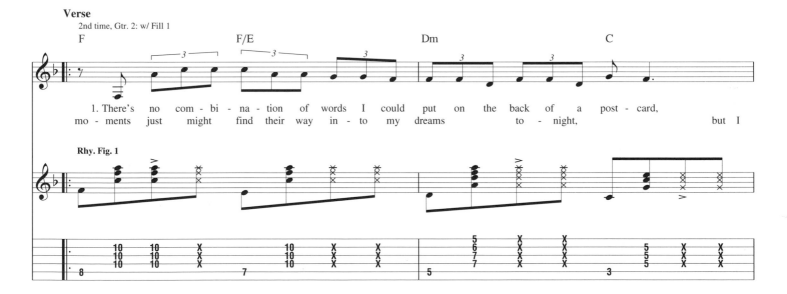

1. There's no com-bi-na-tion of words I could put on the back of a post-card,
mo-ments just might find their way in-to my dreams to-night, but I

Rhy. Fig. 1

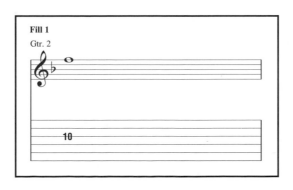

Fill 1
Gtr. 2

4

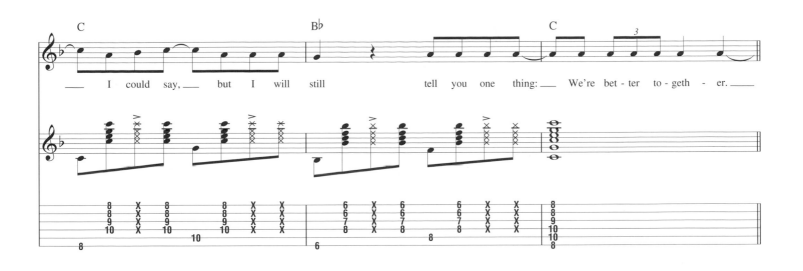

I could say, __ but I will still   tell you one thing: __ We're bet - ter to - geth - er. __

Outro

*Chord symbols reflect implied harmony.

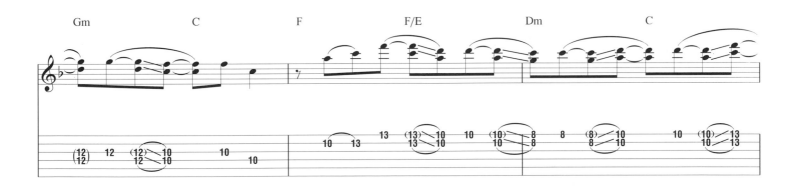

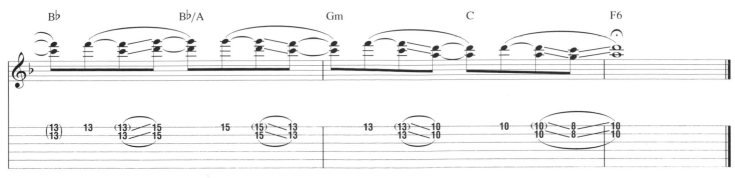

NEVER KNOW

I turn the page___ and read the sto - ry a - gain___ and a - gain and a -
mo - ments just com - bust - ing, feel cer - tain but we'll nev - er nev - er

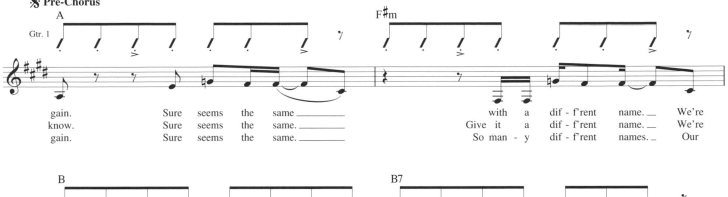

𝄋 Pre-Chorus

Gtr. 1

gain. Sure seems the same_____ with a dif - f'rent name.___ We're
know. Sure seems the same._____ Give it a dif - f'rent name.___ We're
gain. Sure seems the same._____ So man - y dif - f'rent names. _ Our

break - ing and re - build - ing and we're grow - ing, al - ways guess - ing.⎫
beg - ging and we're need - ing and we're try - ing and we're breath - ing.⎬ Nev - er
hearts are strong, our heads are weak, we'll al - ways be com - pet - ing.⎭

Chorus

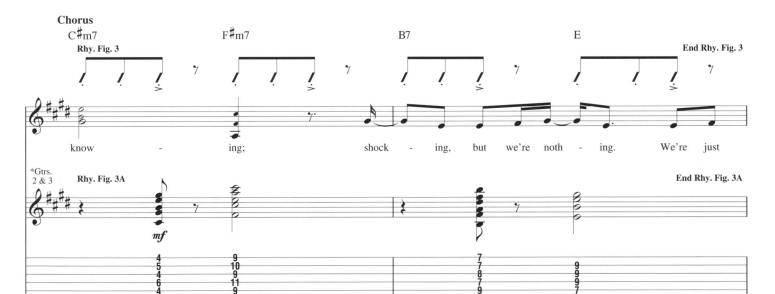

know - ing; shock - ing, but we're noth - ing. We're just

*Acous. gtrs.

Gtr. 1: w/ Rhy. Fig. 3 (3 times)
Gtrs. 2 & 3: w/ Rhy. Fig. 3A (3 times)

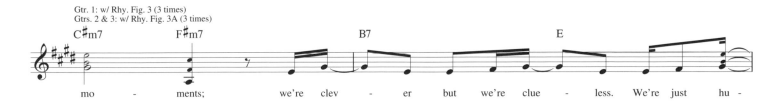

mo - ments; we're clev - er but we're clue - less. We're just hu -

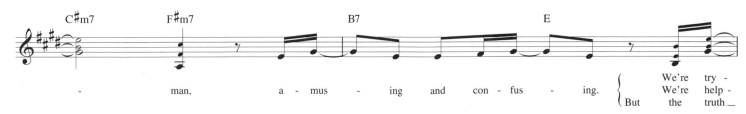

- man, a - mus - ing and con - fus - ing. ⎰ We're try -
⎱ We're help -
But the truth _

- - ing, but where ___ is this all lead - ing? We'll nev - er know. ___
- - ing, we're build -
___ is, all ___

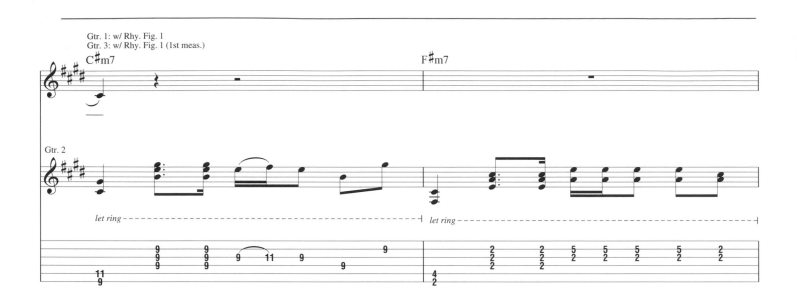

Gtr. 1: w/ Rhy. Fig. 1
Gtr. 3: w/ Rhy. Fig. 1 (1st meas.)

Gtr. 2

let ring -
let ring -

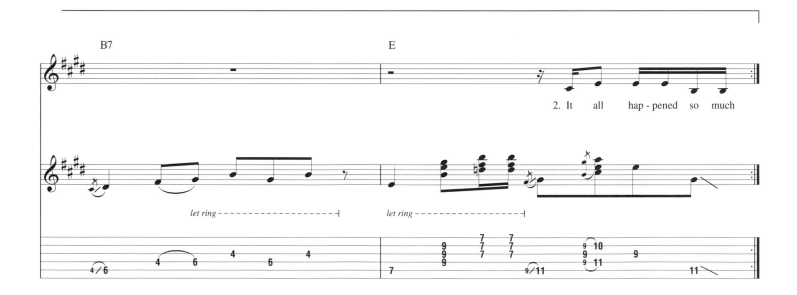

let ring - - - - - - - - - - - -
let ring - - - - - - - - - - - -

2. It all hap - pened so much

Gtrs. 1 & 2: w/ Rhy. Fig. 1
Gtr. 3: w/ Rhy. Fig. 1 (1st meas.)

- - ing and we're grow - ing. Nev - er know. ___
___ we got is ques - tions. We'll nev - er know. ___

You can nev - er know. ___

F#m7   B7   3   E

Nev - er know. _____ Nev - er know. _____

Verse

Gtr. 1: w/ Rhy. Fig. 1

C#m7   F#m7

3. Knock, knock, com - in' door to door; _____ tell ya that their met - a - phor's bet - ter than yours. _ And

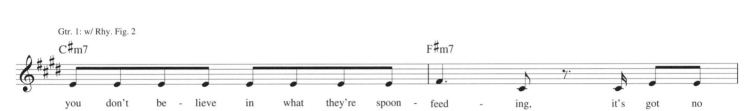

B7   E

you can ei - ther sink or swim, things are look - ing pret - ty grim. If

Gtr. 1: w/ Rhy. Fig. 2

C#m7   F#m7

you don't be - lieve in what they're spoon - feed - ing, it's got no

D.S. al Coda
(take 2nd ending)

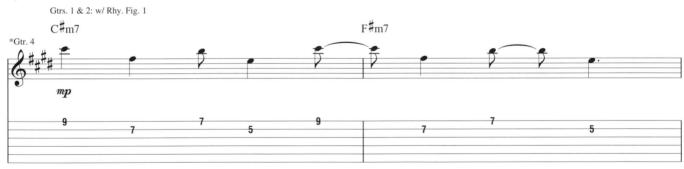

B7   E   E/D#

feel - ing, so I read it a - gain _____ and a - gain and a -

⊕ **Coda**

Gtrs. 1 & 2: w/ Rhy. Fig. 1

C#m7   F#m7

*Gtr. 4

mp

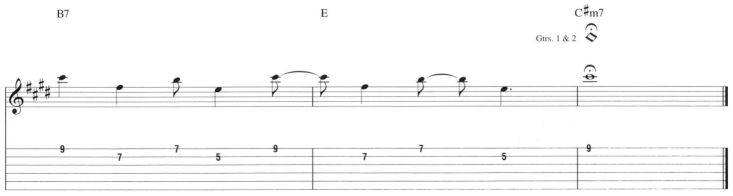

*Piano arr. for gtr.

B7   E   C#m7

Gtrs. 1 & 2

BANANA PANCAKES

Words and Music by
Jack Johnson

Intro
Moderately ♩ = 116

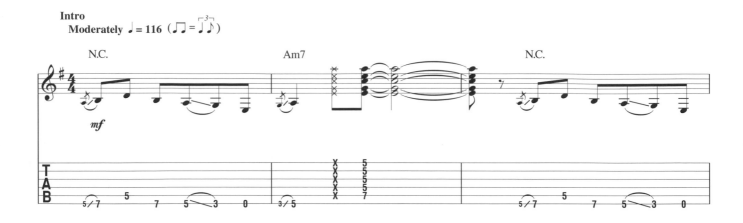

Well, can't you see that it's just rain - ing? ___

There ain't no need to go out - side.   1. But, ba - by, you

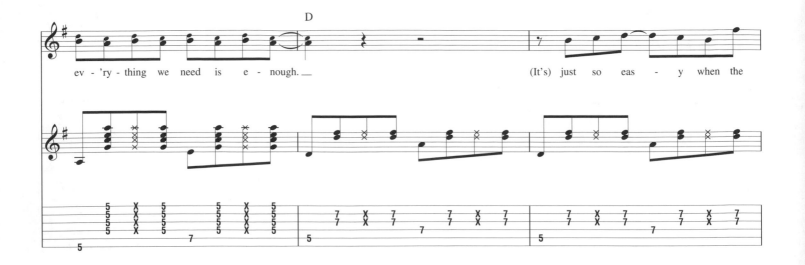

ev - 'ry - thing we need is e - nough. ___ (It's) just so eas - y when the

whole world fits in - side of your arms. ___ Do we real - ly need to pay at - ten - tion
(Oo. ___

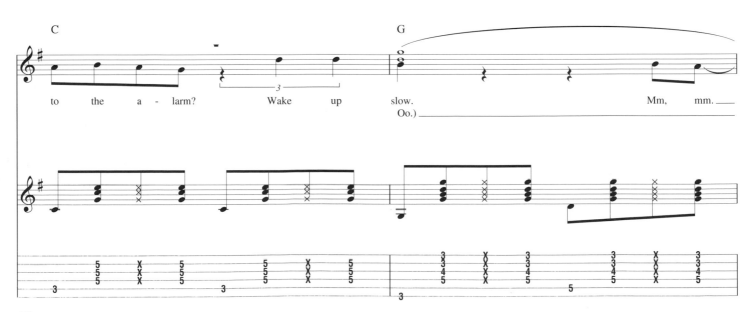

to the a - larm? Wake up slow. Mm, mm. ___
Oo.) ___

GOOD PEOPLE

Words and Music by
Jack Johnson

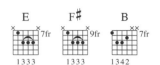

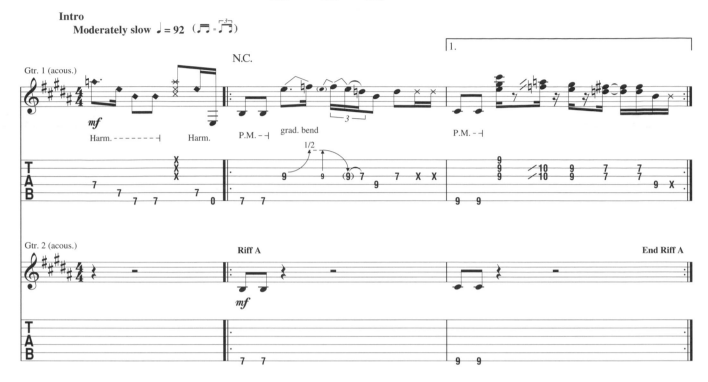

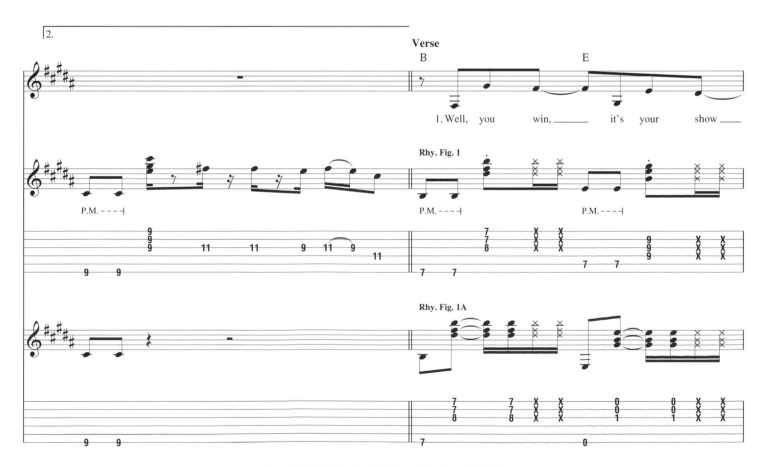

We got heaps and heaps _ of what __ we sow.
2. They got

Verse
Gtrs. 1 & 2: w/ Rhy. Figs. 1 & 1A (4 times)
Gtr. 3: w/ Riff B (4 times)

this and that with a rat‑tle a tat. _ Test‑ing, __ one, two. Man, what‑cha gon‑na do? Bad

news, mis‑used, got too much to lose. Gim‑me some truth, _ now who's _ side are we on? What‑

ev‑er you say. ___ Turn on the boob tube; I'm in the mood to o‑bey. __ So

lead me a‑stray. _____ And by the way ___ now... Where'd all the good peo‑ple

Chorus
Gtrs. 1 & 2: w/ Rhy. Figs. 1 & 1A (4 times)
Gtr. 3: w/ Riff B (4 times)

go? _____ I've been chang‑ing chan‑nels; I don't _

___ see them on the T ‑ V shows. Where'd all the good peo‑ple go? _____

We got heaps and heaps _ of what __ we sow.

1.
2.

Interlude
Gtr. 2: w/ Riff A (2 times)
1st time, Gtr. 3: w/ Riff A (1st meas.)

Gtr. 1
N.C.

P.M. ‑‑‑   grad. bend   P.M. ‑‑   rake ‑‑   P.M. ‑‑

1/2

Bridge

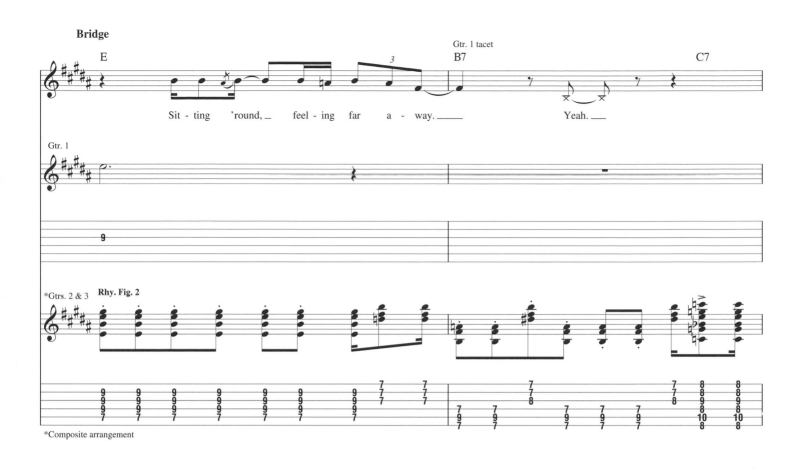

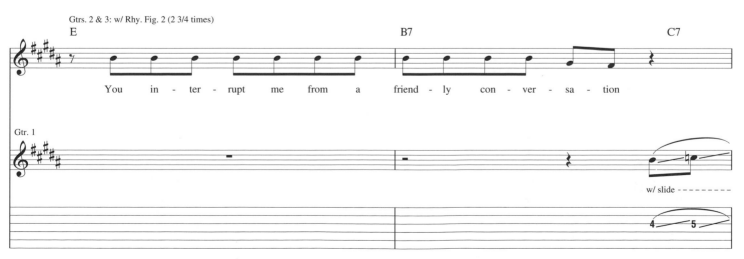

go? _____

End Voc. Fig. 1

We got heaps and heaps _ of what __ we sow.

w/ Voc. Fig. 1

They got this and that with a rat - tle a tat. __ Test - ing, __

__ one, two. Man, what - cha gon - na do? Bad news, mis - used, give me some truth. __ You got

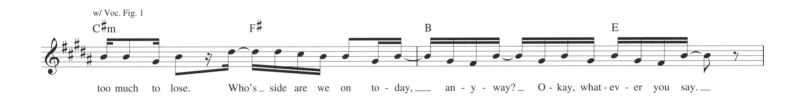

w/ Voc. Fig. 1

too much to lose. Who's _ side are we on to - day, ___ an - y - way? _ O - kay, what - ev - er you say. __

Wrong or res - o - lute but in the mood to o - bey. __ Sta - tion to sta - tion, de - sen - si -

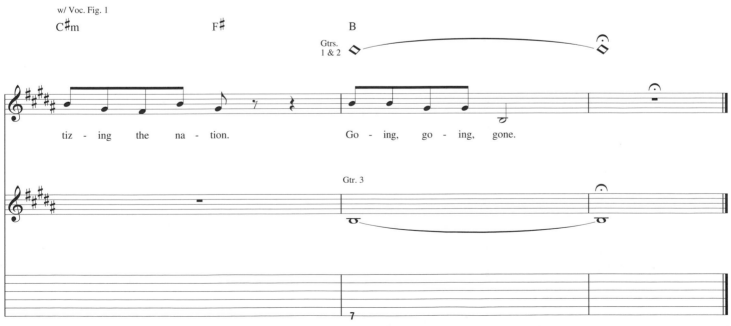

w/ Voc. Fig. 1

tiz - ing the na - tion. Go - ing, go - ing, gone.

NO OTHER WAY

Words and Music by
Jack Johnson

Drop D tuning, capo III:
(low to high) D-A-D-G-B-E

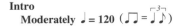

Intro
Moderately ♩ = 120

*All music sounds a minor 3rd higher than indicated due to capo.

**Chord symbols reflect implied harmony.

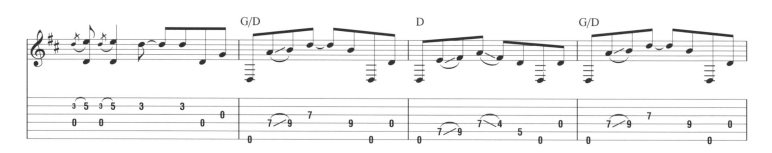

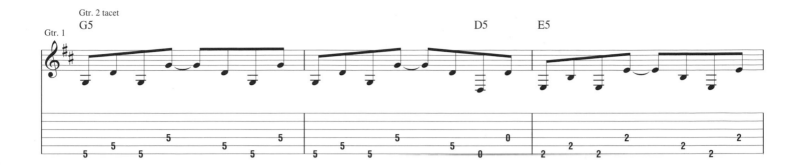

Verse

1. When your mind __ is a mess, __ so is mine. __ I can't sleep __ 'cause it hurts __ when I think. __

__ My thoughts aren't at peace __ with the plans __ that we make, __ chanc - es we take. __

__ They're not yours; __ they're not mine. __ There's waves __ that can break. All the words __ that we said __

__ and the words __ that we mean. __ Words __ can fall short, __ can't see __ the un - seen, __

__ 'cause the world __ is a - wake. __ For some - bod - y's sake __ now, please __ close your eyes; __

25

— wom - an, please — get some sleep. — sleep. } And know — that if I knew all of the an - swers I would —

— not hold — them from you. Know all of the things that I know, — { we 'cause we } told — each oth - er

there is no oth-er way. ____ Mm, ____ mm, ____

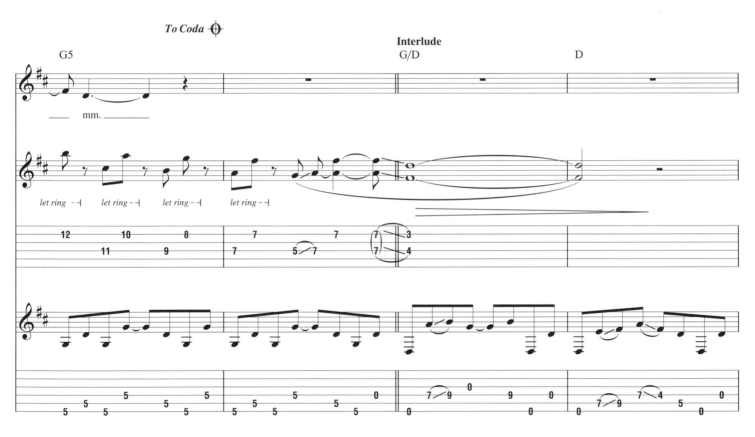

To Coda ⊕

Interlude

____ mm. ____

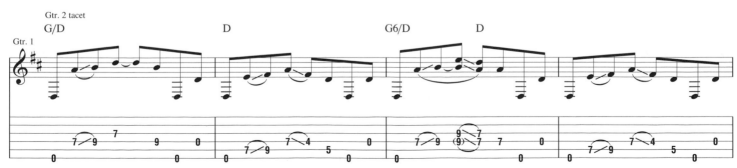

Gtr. 2 tacet

Gtr. 1

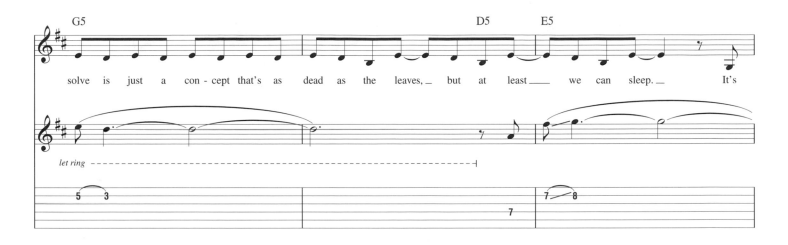

solve is just a con - cept that's as dead as the leaves, __ but at least __ we can sleep. __ It's

D.S. al Coda

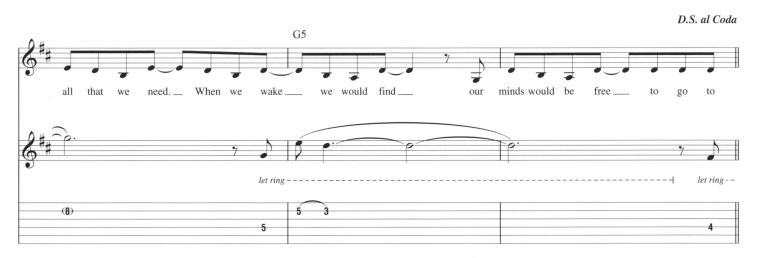

all that we need. __ When we wake __ we would find __ our minds would be free __ to go to

⊕ **Coda**

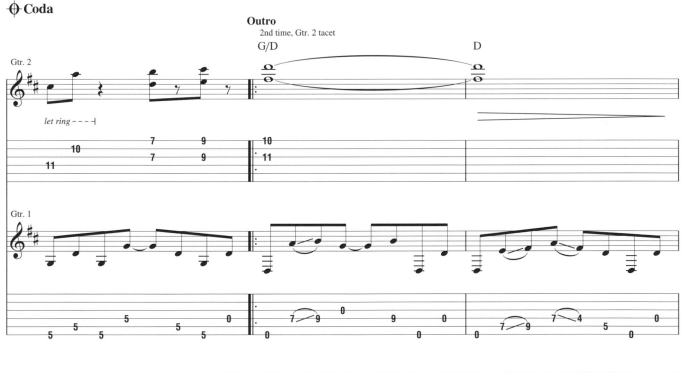

Outro
2nd time, Gtr. 2 tacet

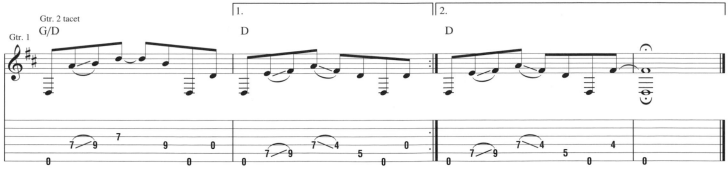

29

SITTING, WAITING, WISHING

Words and Music by
Jack Johnson

F

Won't this plot not twist?_____ I've had e - nough mys - ter - y.____

C   E

Keep build - ing it up,_____ but then you're shoot - ing me down.____

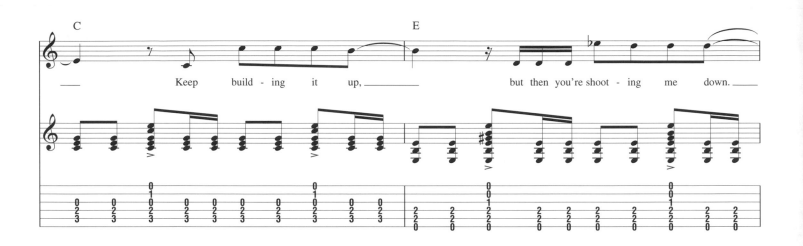

F   G

But I'm al - read - y down;_____ just_____ wait a min - ute.____

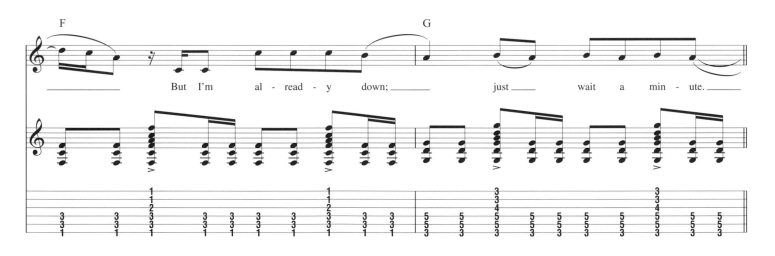

Interlude

Gtr. 1: w/ Rhy. Fig. 1 (2 times)

A5   Am7   G5   G7   F5   F7

Just sit - ting, wait - ing._____

*Gtr. 2

mf

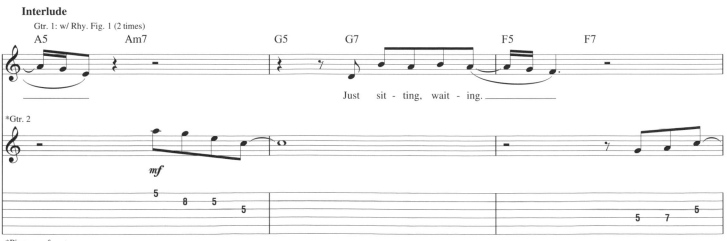

*Piano arr. for gtr.

32

STAPLE IT TOGETHER

Lyrics by
Jack Johnson
Music by
Jack Johnson
and Merlo Podlewski

Intro

Moderately slow ♩ = 100

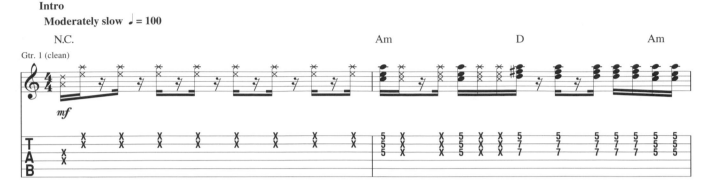

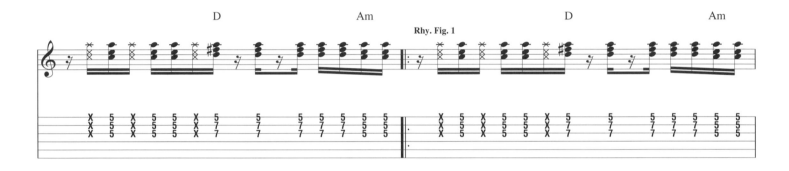

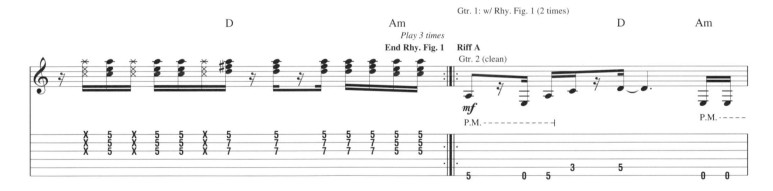

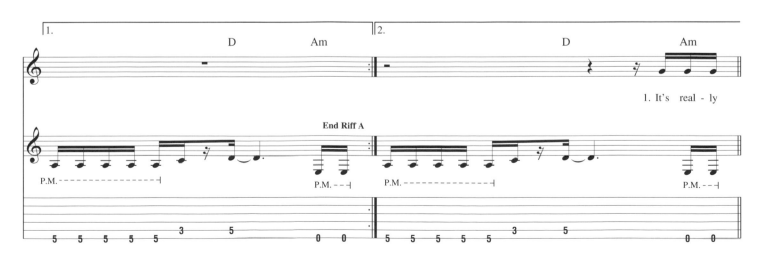

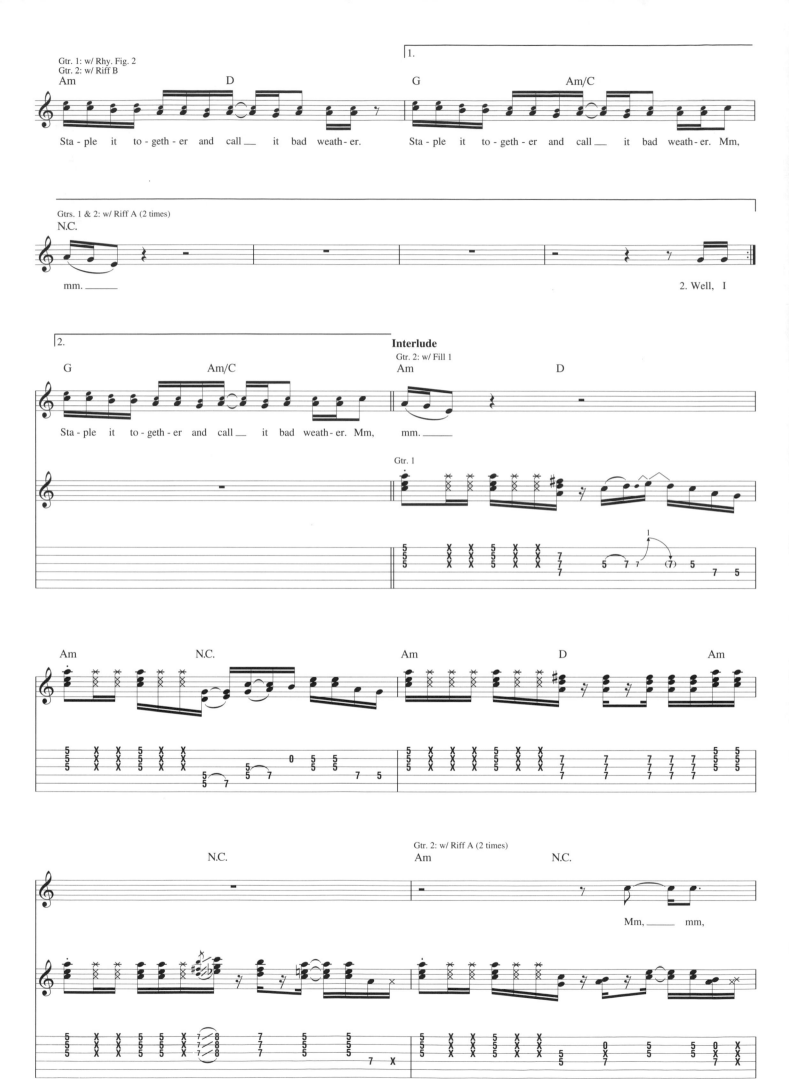

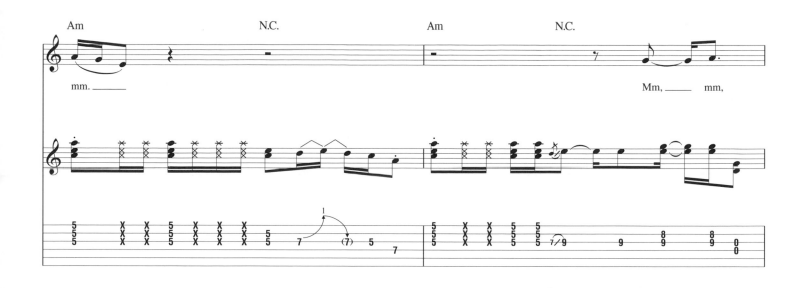

D.S. al Coda
(take 1st lyrics)

⊕ **Coda**

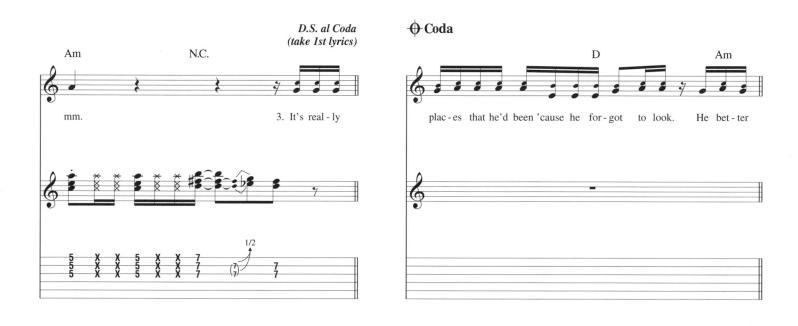

Chorus

Gtr. 1: w/ Rhy. Fig. 2 (4 times)

Gtr. 2: w/ Riff D (3 times)

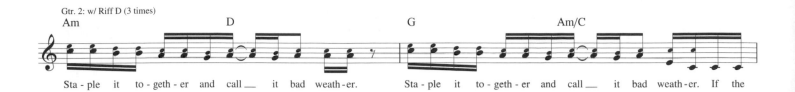

Sta - ple it to - geth - er and call ___ it bad weath - er. Sta - ple it to - geth - er and call ___ it bad weath - er. If the

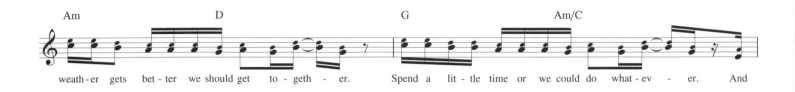

weath - er gets bet - ter we should get to - geth - er. Spend a lit - tle time or we could do what - ev - er. And

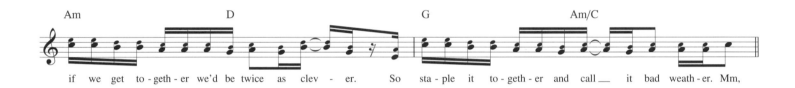

if we get to - geth - er we'd be twice as clev - er. So sta - ple it to - geth - er and call ___ it bad weath - er. Mm,

Outro

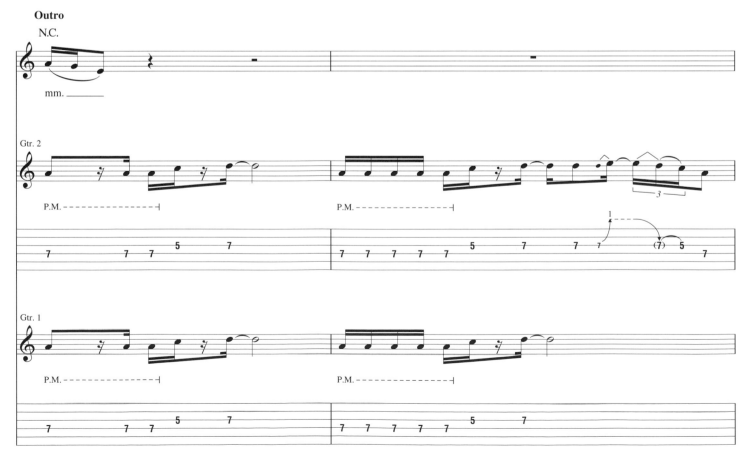

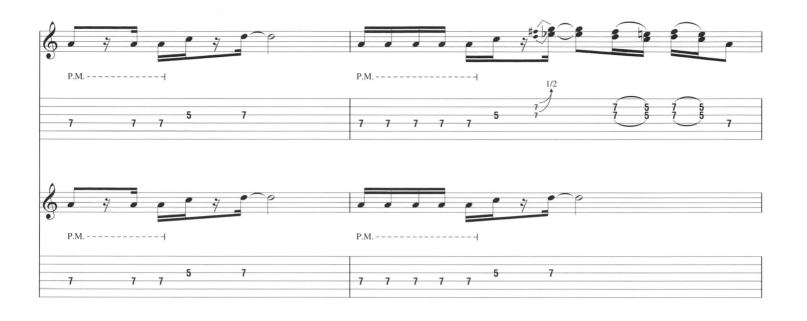

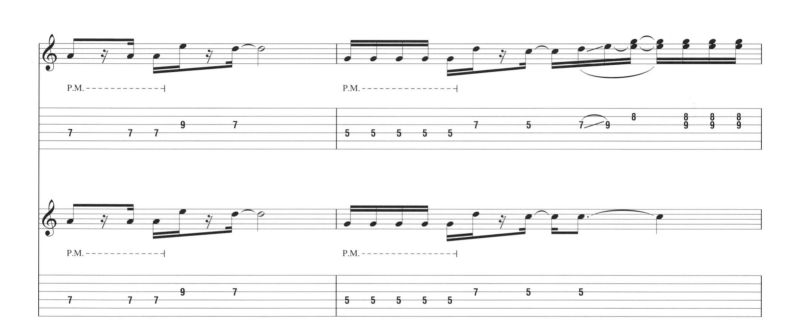

Am7

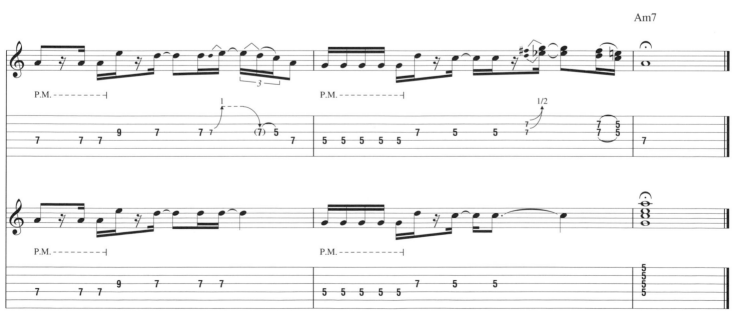

SITUATIONS

Words and Music by
Jack Johnson

*All music sounds a whole step higher than indicated due to capo.

IF I COULD

Words and Music by
Jack Johnson

CRYING SHAME

BREAKDOWN

BELLE

Words and Music by
Jack Johnson

53

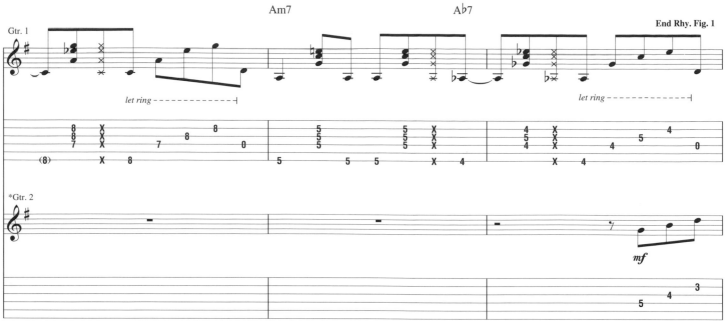

*Accordion arr. for gtr.

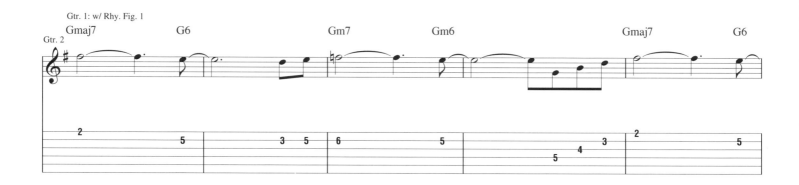

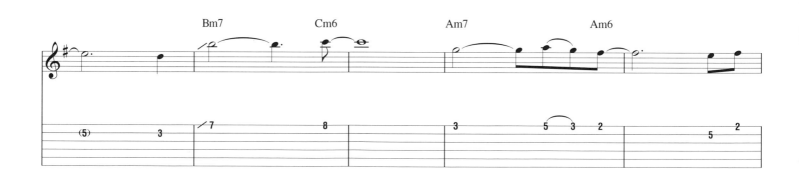

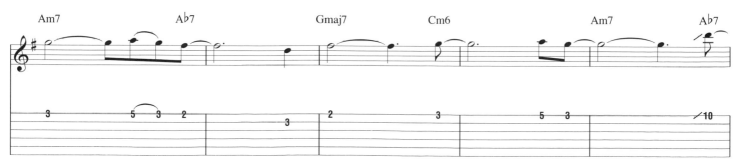

Verse

Gtr. 1: w/ Rhy. Fig. 1 (1st 6 meas.)

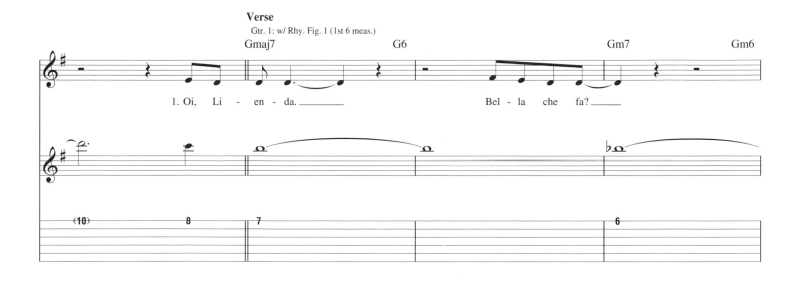

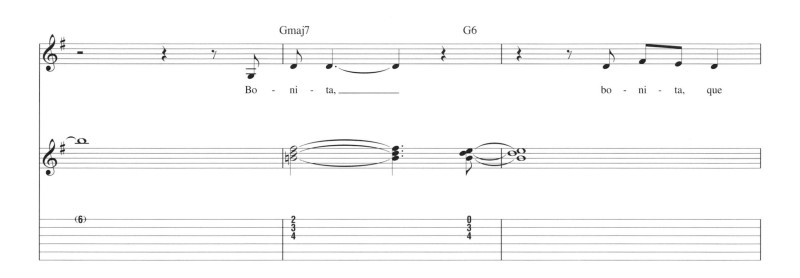

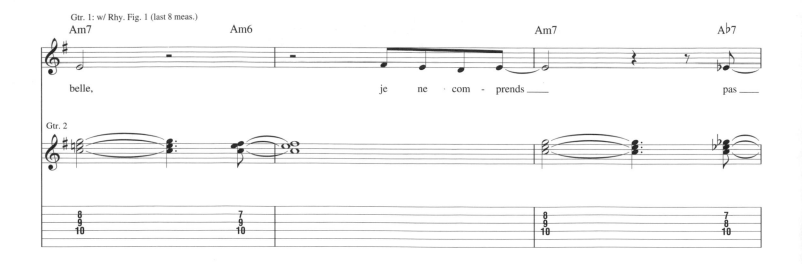

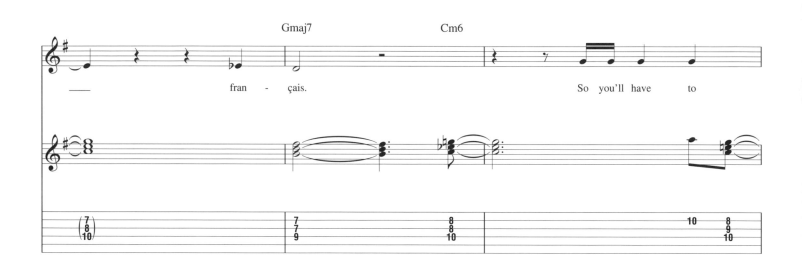

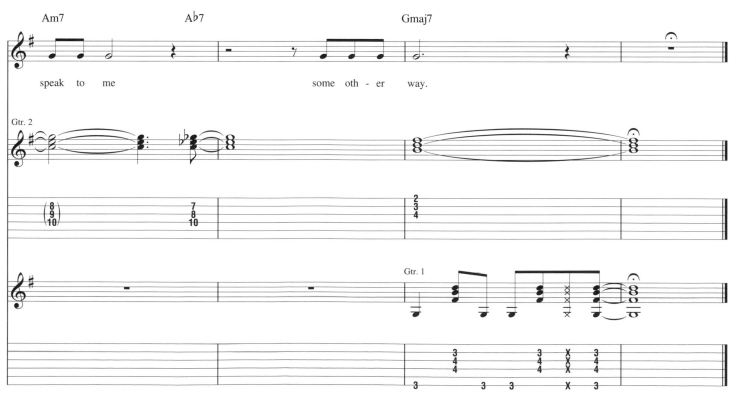

56

DO YOU REMEMBER

Words and Music by
Jack Johnson

Capo II

Intro
Moderately slow, in 2 ♩ = 96

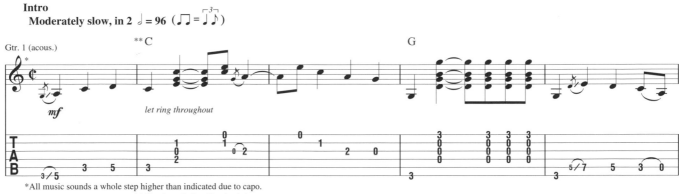

*All music sounds a whole step higher than indicated due to capo.
**Chord symbols reflect basic harmony.

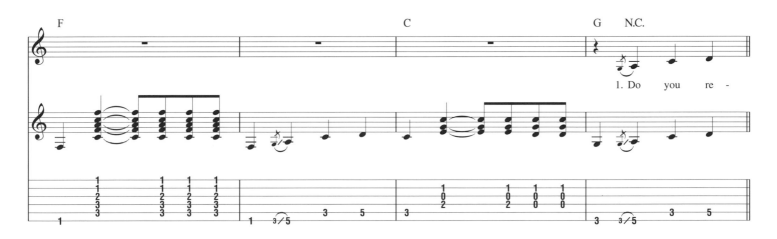

Verse

2nd time, Gtr. 1: w/ Rhy. Fill 1

mem - ber when ____ we first met; I sure do. It was some -
mem - ber when ____ we first moved in to - geth - er? The pi -

Rhy. Fill 1
Gtr. 1

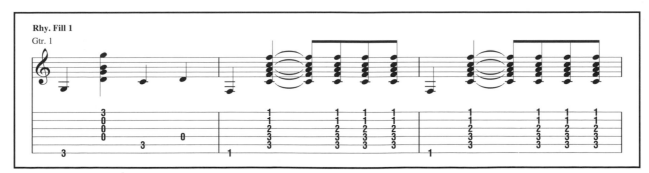

time _____ in _____ ear - ly Sep - tem - ber.
an - o - took up the liv - ing room.
Well, you were
You'd play me

la - zy a - bout _____ it; you made me wait a - round.
boog - ie - woog - ie; I'd play you love songs.
I was so
You'd say we're

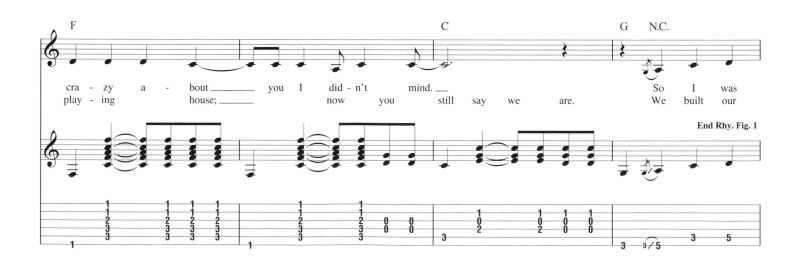

cra - zy a - bout _____ you I did - n't mind. _____
play - ing house; _____ now you still say we are.
So I was
We built our

Gtr. 1: w/ Rhy. Fig. 1 (1 7/8 times)

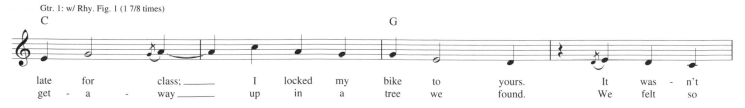

late for class; _____ I locked my bike to yours.
get a - way _____ up in a tree we found.
It was - n't
We felt so

58

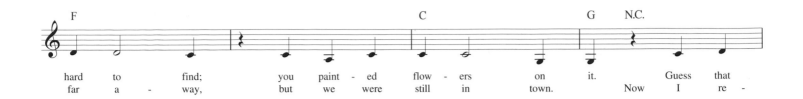

hard to find; you paint-ed flow-ers on it. Guess that
far a-way, but we were still in town. Now I re-

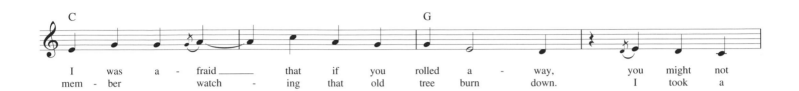

I was a-fraid _____ that if you rolled a-way, you might not
mem-ber watch-ing that old tree burn down. I took a

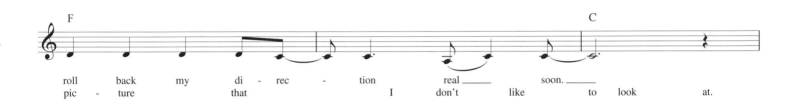

roll back my di-rec-tion real _____ soon. _____
pic-ture my that I don't like to look at.

Chorus

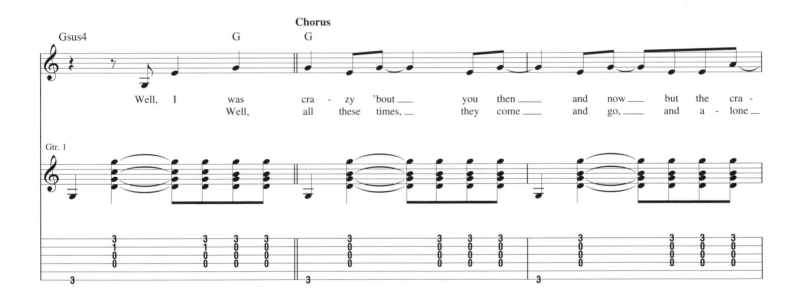

Gtr. 1

Well, I was cra-zy 'bout _____ you then _____ and now _____ but the cra-
Well, all these times, _____ they come _____ and go, _____ and a-lone _____

-zi-est thing of all, _____ o-ver ten years _____
don't seem so long, _____ o-ver ten years _____

have gone _____ by _____
have gone _____ by.

and you're _ still
We can't _ re -

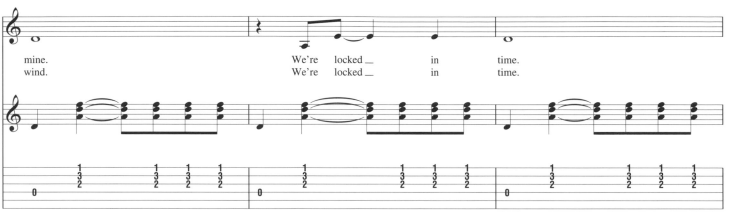

mine.
wind.

We're locked _ in time.
We're locked _ in time.

Let's _ re - wind. _____
But you're _ still mine. _____

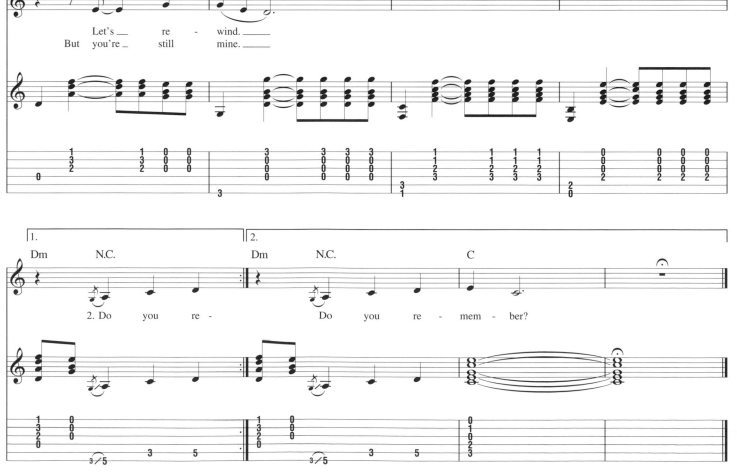

2. Do you re -
Do you re - mem - ber?

CONSTELLATIONS

It's get-ting late. ____

Chorus

It was just an-oth-er night ____

with the sun-set and ____ a ____ moon-rise

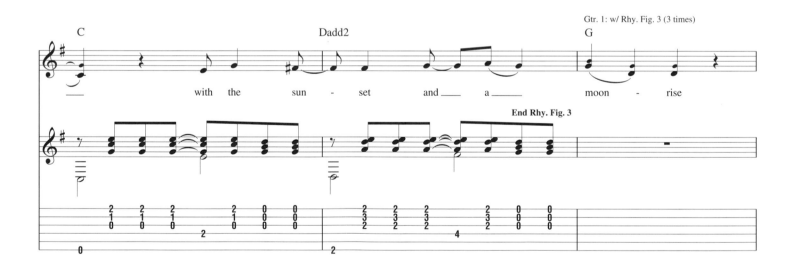

not so far ____ be-hind ____ to give us just ____ e-nough ____ light to

lay ____ down un-der-neath ____ the stars, ____ lis-ten to {Pa — pa's / all ____ the} trans-la-tions

*Upstemmed notes strummed w/ index finger, till Outro.

D.S. al Coda

way.

⊕ Coda

Outro

Gtr. 1: w/ Rhy. Fig. 1 (1 1/2 times)

**Strum w/ index finger.